Chris J's Magni

A Journey Through Emotions

Stacey Lloyd Ph.D

Copyright © 2024 by Stacey Y Lloyd Ph.D.

All rights reserved. No part of this book may be reproduced in any form without permission from the author or publisher, except as a permitted by U.S. copyright law. To request permission, contact Dr. Lloyd @ jyvonne2007@gmail.com.

Printed in The United States of America
Designed by Sarah Artista

Chris J loved spending afternoons with his friend Devonte, drawing pictures in the park. One day, Chris J was feeling on top of the world. He had passed his math test and his drawing was coming along perfectly.

But then, a strong wind blew his drawing sheet away.
Frustration bubbled up inside Chris J.

He clenched his fists and furrowed his brow.

Mrs. Lloyd, who was nearby, overheard their conversation. She smiled warmly and walked over. "Chris J," Mrs. Lloyd said kindly, "it sounds like you're feeling frustrated. That's okay, everyone feels frustrated sometimes."

Chris J looked up, surprised. "But how do I stop feeling this way?"

Mrs. Lloyd pointed to her head. "The key is right up here, Chris J, in your magnificent mind!" she explained. "Your brain is like a supercomputer, helping you think and feel."

She then explained that Chris J's frustration was a signal, letting him know he was upset about the lost drawing. "Just like we can control our bodies," Mrs. Lloyd continued, "we can also learn to control our emotions with a little practice."

Mrs. Lloyd taught Chris J some calming down techniques. They took slow, deep breaths together, imagining their frustration melting away like snowflakes.

Chris J felt the tension ease from his shoulders.

Devonte joined in, suggesting they draw a new picture together. Chris J smiled. He realized that even though Chris J felt frustrated, he could choose how to react.

Together, they created an even more fantastic drawing, filled with vibrant colors and their favorite superheroes. Chris J beamed with pride.

He had used his magnificent mind to navigate his emotions and create something wonderful with his friend.
From that day on, Chris J paid more attention to his feelings. He learned that his emotions were messengers, giving him clues about how he was feeling. And most importantly, he learned that he had the power to manage his emotions and use his brain to create a happy and fulfilling life.

Chris J's

Magnificent Mind tells a story about a bright and inquisitive boy who felt the emotion of frustration and learned that the brain is a supercomputer that helps us think and feel and allows us to make positive choices for a more fulfilling life.

Chris J's Journey

A Colorful Day on Astor Street in Newark New Jersey.

Stacey Lloyd Ph.D

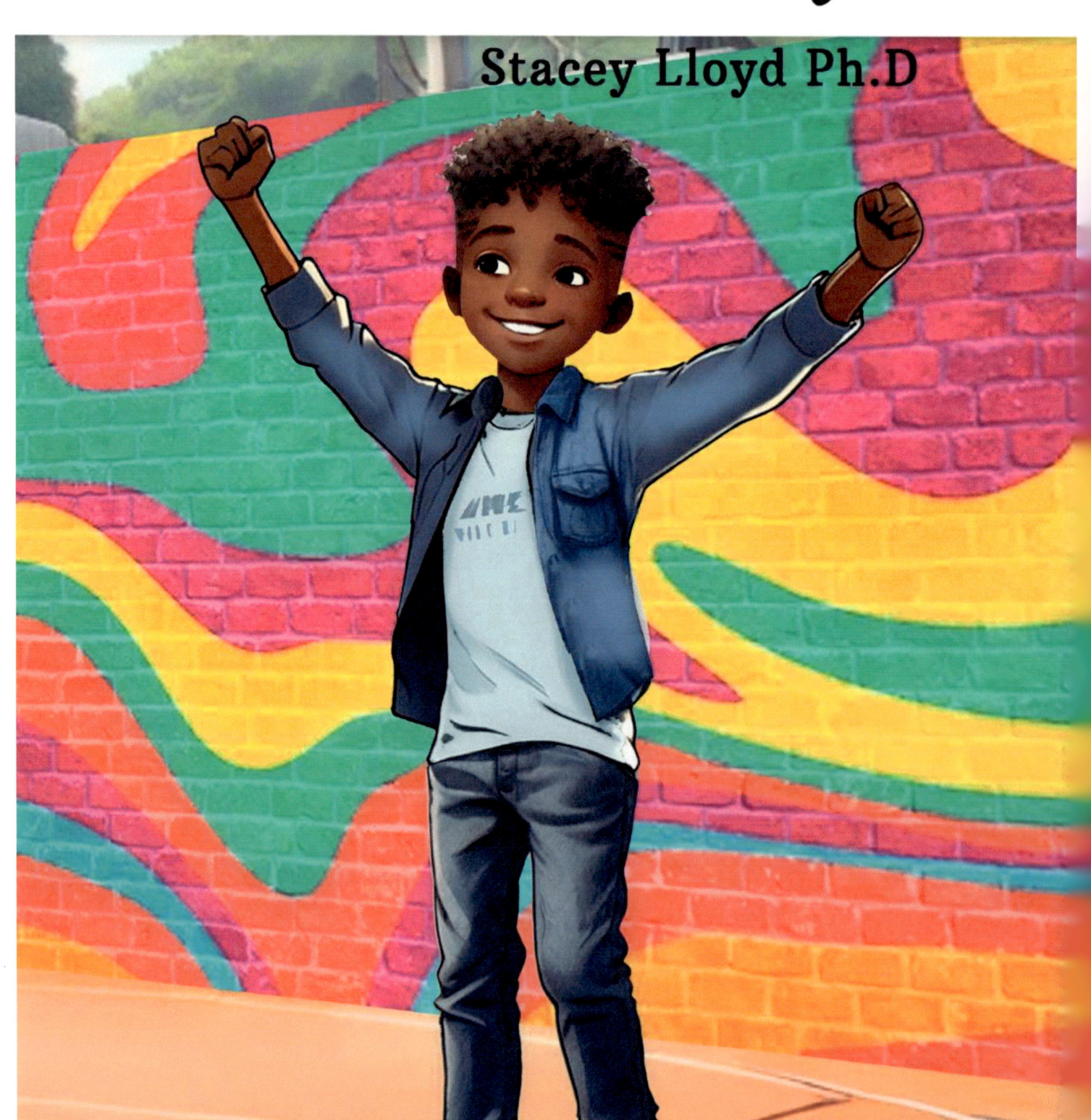

Chris J bounces out of bed, ready to start his day in his hometown of Newark, New Jersey.

But as he steps outside, a frown replaces his smile. The colorful mural he and his friends painted on the playground wall is covered in graffiti. Disappointment washes over Chris J.

He clenches his fists.
Anger bubbles up inside.

He wants to yell and scream, but then he remembers what Mrs. Lloyd teaches in class: take a deep breath. Chris J closes his eyes and inhales slowly, counting to five. He exhales slowly, counting to ten.

Feeling a little better, Chris J looks around. His cousin Devonte is just as upset (sadness). Together, they decide to fix the mural.

They grab paintbrushes and buckets.

Mixing colors that reflect the joy of their community (cooperation).

Chris J and Devonte finish the mural, even brighter and more beautiful than before. They step back, feeling proud of what they have accomplished (pride).

Chris J realizes that even in Newark, New Jersey where there are challenges, there is the power of friendship and positive emotions.

Chris J's Amazing Kite

A Story About Reaching for Dreams

Stacey Lloyd Ph.D

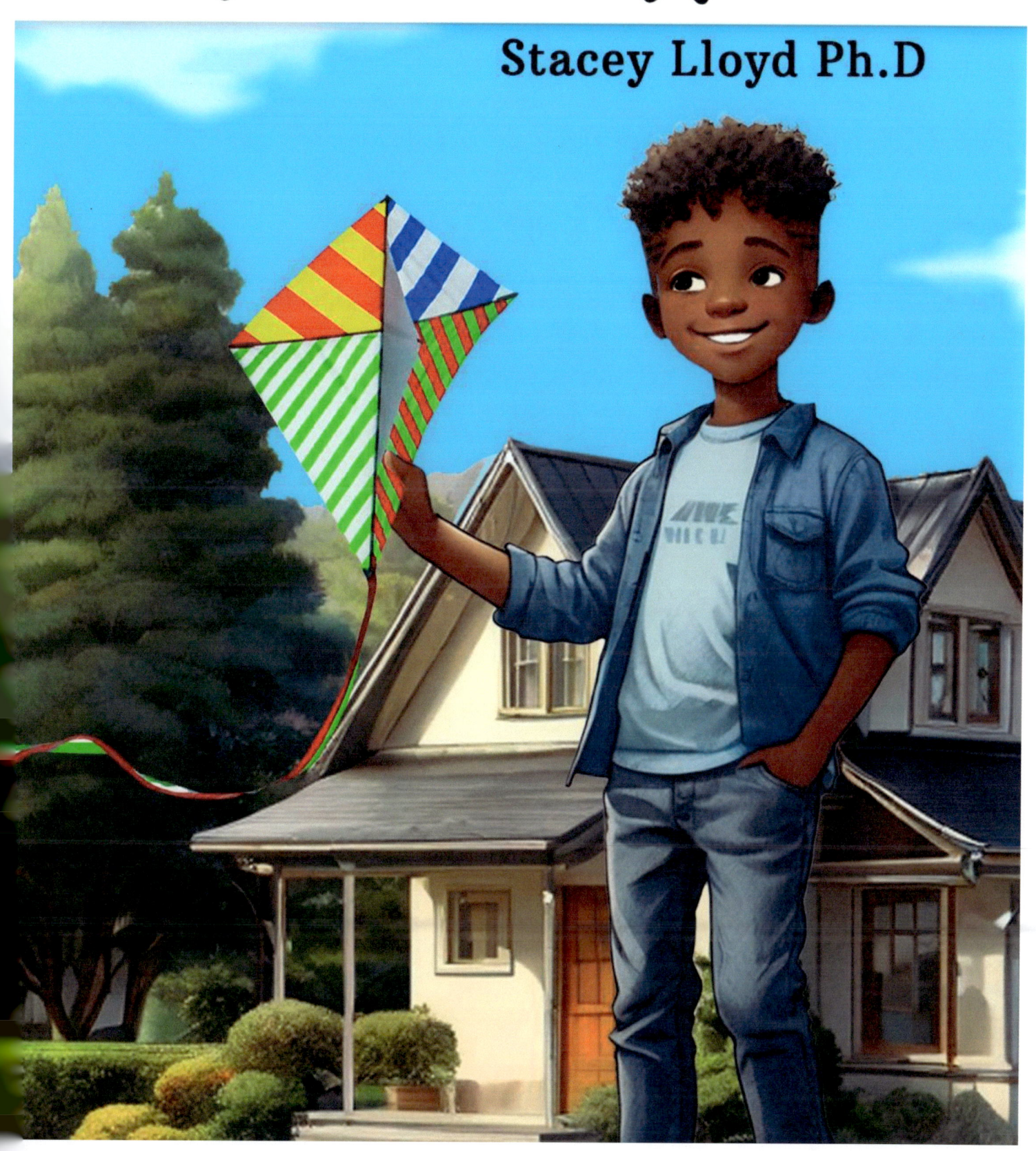

Chris J loved spending afternoons with his dad, building amazing things out of cardboard boxes and bottle caps. But lately, things felt different at home. Dad wasn't around as much, and there wasn't as much laughter. A dark cloud seemed to hang over their house (trauma).

At school, Chris J found himself daydreaming during lessons. Mrs. Lloyd, his teacher, noticed his change in mood. One day, she gently asked Chris J if something was bothering him. Chris J hesitated, then confided in Mrs. Lloyd about the situation at home. Mrs. Lloyd listened patiently, then offered a warm smile. "Even when things are tough, Chris J," she said, "there's always strength and hope inside you."

She then showed Chris J a picture of a hot air balloon soaring high above a field of colorful wildflowers. "What if you could set a goal, a dream you'd like to work towards?" Mrs. Lloyd asked.

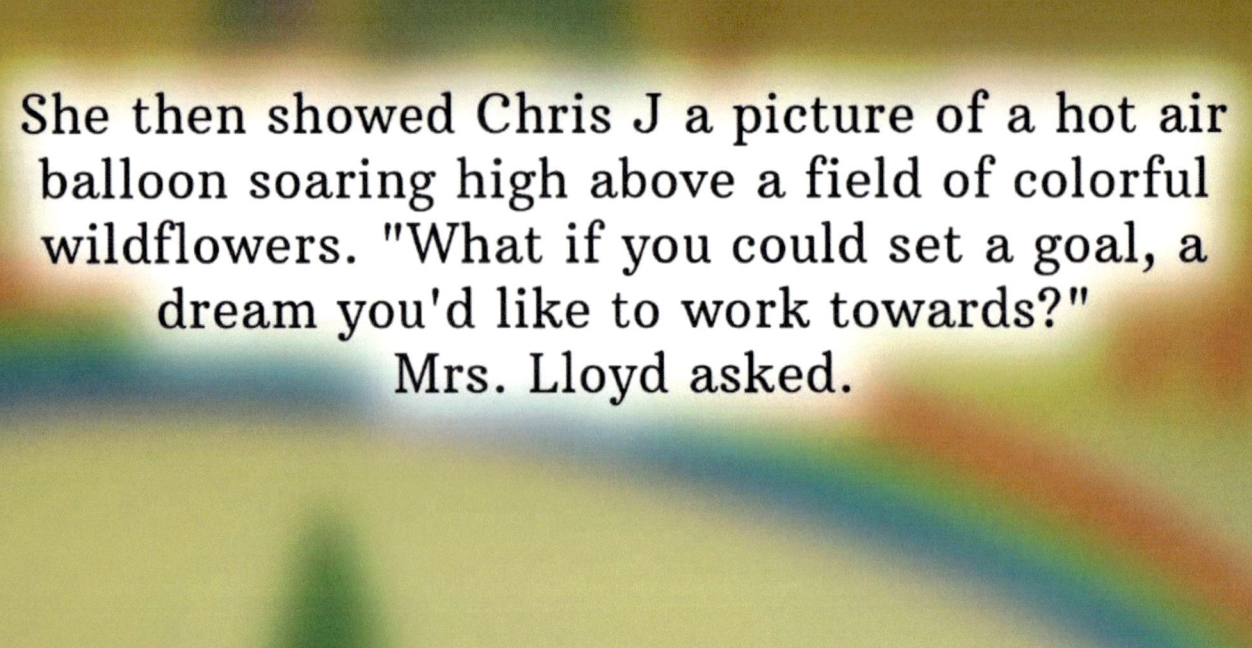

Excited, Chris J started brainstorming. He drew sketches of his dream kite, listing the materials he'd need. He even practiced making small paper kites with Mrs. Lloyd's help.

One sunny afternoon, Dad finally came home. Chris J, with a hopeful smile, showed him his plans for the giant kite. Dad's eyes welled up with pride. "That's amazing, son!" he boomed, ruffling Chris J's hair.

Together, Dad and Chris J collected materials, laughing and sharing stories as they built. Even though things were still difficult at home, Chris J felt a spark of joy he hadn't felt in a while.

Finally, the day arrived to fly their creation. Chris J stood proudly beside his dad as the wind carried their magnificent kite high above the park, a burst of colors against the clear blue sky (achievement).

Looking up at the soaring kite, Chris J realized that even during tough times, he could still reach for his dreams. He had the strength inside him, the support of his loved ones, and the power to set goals that brought him hope and happiness.

Chris J's

Amazing Kite details his struggles with trauma brought on by longing for his father's presence. He realized everything is achievable with the correct attitude, good planning, and faith.

Chris J's Special Treasure Box

A Story About Healing Feelings

Stacey Lloyd Ph.D

Chris J loved spending time with his mother Momma Lloyd. One day, while rummaging through the attic, Chris J discovered a dusty, old treasure box. Inside, nestled amongst seashells and colorful pebbles, were beautiful sparkling stones.

"What are these, mom?" Chris J asked, holding up a smooth, gray stone.

Momma Lloyd smile faded a little. "Those are memory stones, Chris J," she explained. "Each one holds a feeling or a memory."

Chris J noticed another stone, dark and rough. "What about this one?" he asked hesitantly. Momma Lloyd took a deep breath. "That stone," she said gently, "holds a sad memory, a time when I felt scared and alone."

Chris J's brow furrowed with concern. "But Momma Lloyd, you are always so strong." Momma Lloyd chuckled softly. "Everyone experiences tough times, sweetheart. It's okay to feel sad or scared sometimes."

She explained that difficult experiences can leave strong emotions behind, like the rough stone. But just like the smooth stone, happy memories could exist too.

Chris J understood. He thought about a time he felt scared during a thunderstorm. But he also remembered the joy of spending that same day playing board games with Momma Lloyd.
"So, we can have both happy and sad feelings?" Chris J asked.

Momma Lloyd nodded. "Yes, and that's okay. But sometimes, the sad feelings can feel overwhelming, like a big storm cloud."

She then showed Chris J a special technique. They closed their eyes and imagined placing the rough stone inside a sparkling bubble of light. The light, Momma Lloyd explained, represented their strength and love.

Chris J felt a sense of calm wash over him. He realized that even though sad feelings existed, they didn't have to control him. He had the tools to manage them, just like Momma Lloyd.

From that day on, Chris J thought of her feelings as his special treasure box. Some stones held happy memories, others held sad ones. But Chris J knew that with his own inner light, he could navigate his emotions and create a bright and beautiful future.

Chris J found that old treasures can bring happy memories. He also learned that sad feelings are real, but they do not have to control him. He had the tools to take care of his feelings. Chris J thought of how his mother made him feel like a special treasure chest. A few stones held happy memories and some held sad ones. Chris J knew his inner light was his hidden treasure and this treasure would help him to create a wonderful future.

Bullied for my beauty!

Beautiful Colors

Stacey Lloyd Ph.D

Madison and Chris J were best friends. Madison had eyes that were blue like water and she has light brown hair that curled so beautifully. Chris J, had black hair and nice brown eyes. They were an unusual pair, but their differences made their friendship even more special.

There was a student at school that enjoyed picking on others. The student noticed Madison and Chris J right away.
"Hey, look at the mixed-up twins," he sneered.

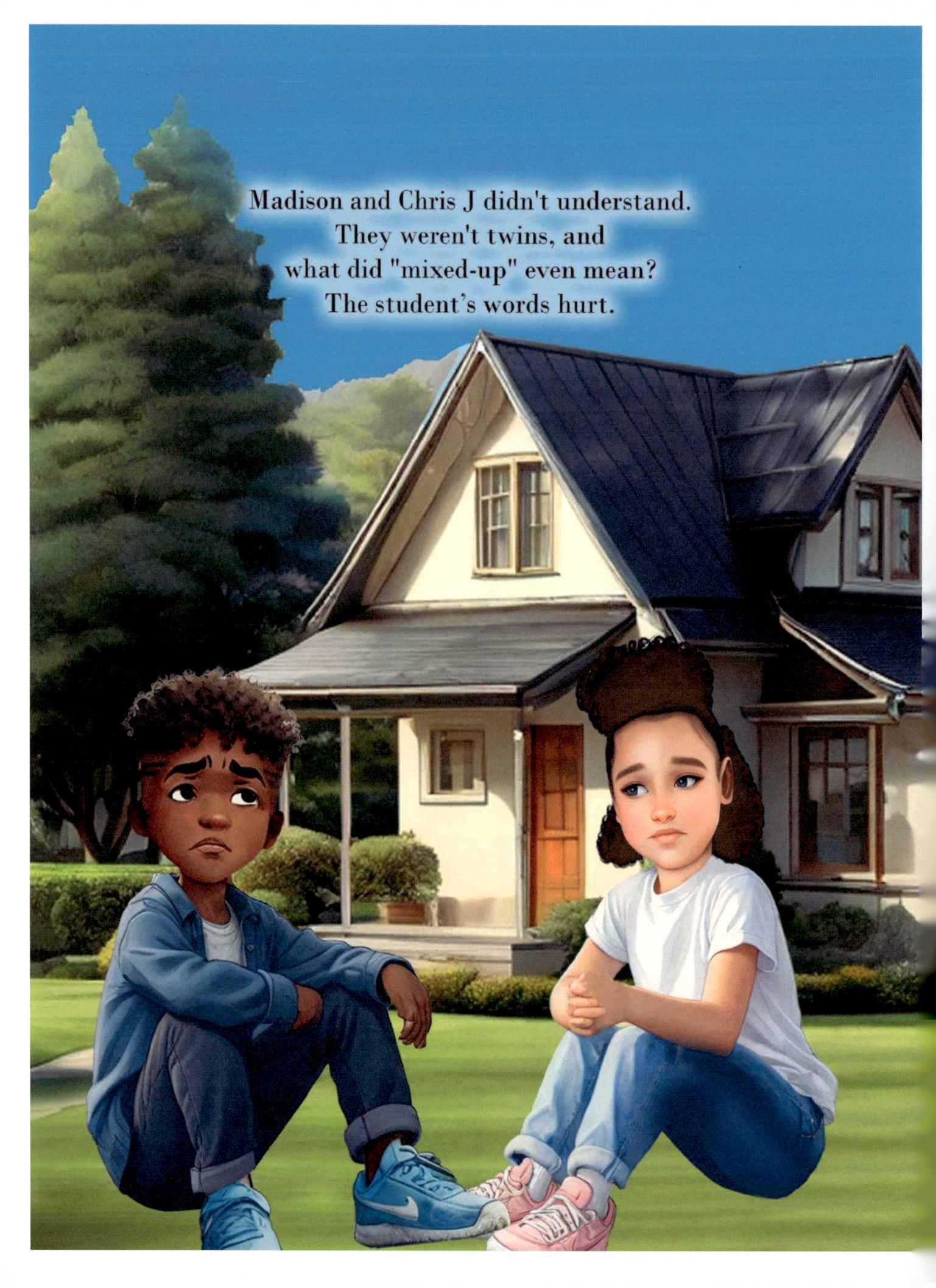

Madison and Chris J didn't understand.
They weren't twins, and
what did "mixed-up" even mean?
The student's words hurt.

The bullying continued. The student would call them names on the playground and push them when they walked in the hallway. Madison and Chris J tried to ignore him, but it was so hard. They started to feel ashamed and sad about their different look.

One afternoon, Madison asked Chris J to walk with her to their teacher Mrs. Lloyd's classroom. When they arrived, Madison could not stop crying. Mrs. Lloyd knelt before her and tucked a strand of Madison's hair behind her ear.
"Your hair is beautiful, Madison," she said. "Just like the way the sunset paint's the sky with all sorts of colors."

Mrs. Lloyd helped both Madison and Chris J to understand that their differences were what made them special. They were like walking rainbows, a beautiful blend of sunshine.

The next day, when the student started his taunts, Madison and Chris J held their heads high.

"We are proud of who we are," Chris J said firmly.

"Our heart shines beautifully," Madison added.

The student looked at them, surprised.
No one had ever stood up to him before.
He mumbled something in a low tone
and walked away.

Madison and Chris J learned that they are beautiful, smart, friendly, and purposeful. They realized that their amazing character was displayed to their classmate and their friendship was a beautiful masterpiece. And from that day on, whenever anyone made a rude comment,
Madison and Chris J would simply smile and say, "We are beautifully fashioned."

Devonte's Backpack

Stacey Lloyd Ph.D

Devonte clutched the worn, leather backpack tightly, its strap digging into his shoulder. It was the only constant in his life, a silent companion through four different foster homes. Inside, hidden between worn comic books and a broken red fire truck, was a faded photograph of his family, frozen in a moment of time. It was a stark contrast to the storm brewing in his stomach as he approached Miller Street Middle School in Newark, New Jersey. New school. New faces. The usual dread coiled in his gut. He hoped, for the hundredth time, that this time would be different.

Lunch was the worst. The cafeteria buzzed with a disharmony of chatter, laughter, and the clatter of trays. Devonte, ever the wallflower, retreated to a corner table, hunching over his peanut butter sandwich.

"Hey, foster boy!"
A voice dripping with venom shattered the quiet. Devonte looked up to see a Rajuan who thought it was okay to bully. Standing by was Chris J looking to confront this bully. Rajuan, burning a conceit that made Devonte want to crawl under the table, slammed a carton of milk onto his tray.
"Spilled your precious lunch, huh? Looks like you can use some help, charity case."
Before Devonte could react, Chris J walked over and helped Devonte with the food that had spilled on the floor.

The Rajuan grabbed Devonte's backpack. Laughter erupted from the students in the cafeteria. Devonte lunged,
a desperate cry escaping his lips.
"Hey! Leave it alone!"
Rajuan held the bag high, an aggressive look in his eyes.
"What's in here, foster boy? Secrets of how to mooch off the system?"
The photo peeked out from a loose zipper. Panic choked Devonte. He lunged again, this time connecting with Rajuan's shoulder. The bag tumbled to the floor, photograph clattering out.
Laughter turned to jeering shouts.
"Look at the foster boy! Misses his mommy?"

Devonte felt tears sting his eyes. He scrambled for the picture, ignoring the spilled milk soaking his lunch. Chris J shoved Rajuan back, the photo slipping out of their reach.

"Whoa, is that your real family? Must be rough, having them throw you away."

The words struck like a physical blow. Devonte snatched the photo, clutching it to his chest. He ran. Didn't stop until he burst through the school doors, ignoring the concerned calls of Mrs. Lloyd.

He found himself in the janitor's closet, a dusty haven. Huddled on a rickety chair, he wept, the photo damp with his tears.
"Hey, kiddo, you alright?"
A gentle voice startled him. It was Mrs. Lloyd, the kind teacher who always seemed to appear when Devonte needed a quiet moment.

Devonte exclaimed how he was always bullied because he did not have a permanent home. He also explained that he carried around his old bookbag from foster home to foster home and never had a real suitcase to place his most precious items in. Mrs. Lloyd explained to him that the true treasure lies in his heart and in his mind. She advised him that she will assist him with getting a new bookbag that he calls his own.

The next day Mrs. Lloyd and many of the school personnel had a major surprise for Devonte hidden in Mrs. Lloyd's personal office. When he walked in, to his surprise he had a brand-new black bookbag with his first and last name engraved on it. They provided him a new suitcase with his initials and the words "hidden treasures" engraved.

They placed a frame with the picture of his mother inside. They filled the suitcase with new socks, t-shirts, notebooks, pens, new pair of sneakers and a nice spring jacket. Devonte was filled with joy. He thanked all of the administrators and assured them that he will work hard in school so that he could be a teacher one day like Mrs. Lloyd.

He left the office with his new bookbag, new sneakers and a sense of confidence. When he walked past Rejuan, in the hallway, Rajuan yelled look at the foster kid, Devonte proudly stated, "I foster love, success, creativity, and peace in my new found treasure, which is my heart." Rejuan softly chuckled but was surprised that Devonte walked away so confidently. Devonte continued to class with a smile that lit up the hallway.

Chris J's friend Bless

Stacey Lloyd Ph.D

Chris J had a close companion named Bless. Bless seemed to have a unique presence among his classmates. Bless was truly remarkable. What set Bless apart from the rest? Bless's family physician diagnosed him with autism when he was just two years old.

He found the noise in the cafeteria, the constant changes in classroom discussions, and the crowded hallways to be quite bothersome. His brain was wired in a way that processed the world in a truly unique manner. Bless was given the nickname "Weird Bless" by some kids. They would play pranks on him, hide his backpack, or make mean comments that he didn't fully grasp.

creating a lively atmosphere that was quite different from the peaceful world he typically enjoyed. He refrained from retaliating; he seemed unfamiliar with the rules of that game. Instead, he kindly knelt to pick up his scattered belongings, his face displaying a hint of confusion.

One day, while Bless was getting ready for recess, a sudden push from behind caused his books to go flying. Laughter filled the air.

Mrs. Lloyd, being a caring teacher, noticed the incident. She knelt beside Bless, her hand gently resting on his shoulder. "Bless," she said gently, her voice a soothing presence amidst the chaos of the playground, "someone was not very nice." I'm sorry, but that's not okay. Chris J joined the conversation and kindly explained to Bless that the bullying behavior was not acceptable.

Bless looked up, his eyes reflecting a sense of confusion.

Mrs. Lloyd and Chris J provided a clear explanation of bullying, using easy-to-understand language and a compassionate approach. Mrs. Lloyd shared advice on the importance of advocating for oneself and seeking support from trusted individuals, such as a friend like Chris J. It was a detailed explanation, but Bless attentively listened, gradually understanding the concept.

The following day, the same group attempted their usual antics. Chris J observed Bless's reaction with interest. However, this time, Bless remained strong. He stood confidently, his voice gentle yet resolute, "Stop it," he said.

Change didn't happen all at once. There were still challenging days, moments when the world felt overwhelmingly, too busy. Bless was making progress and his friend Chris J remained by his side, offering unwavering support. Bless discovered the value of finding peaceful spots during recess, utilizing visual aids to express himself when words weren't enough, and, above all, reaching out for assistance when necessary.

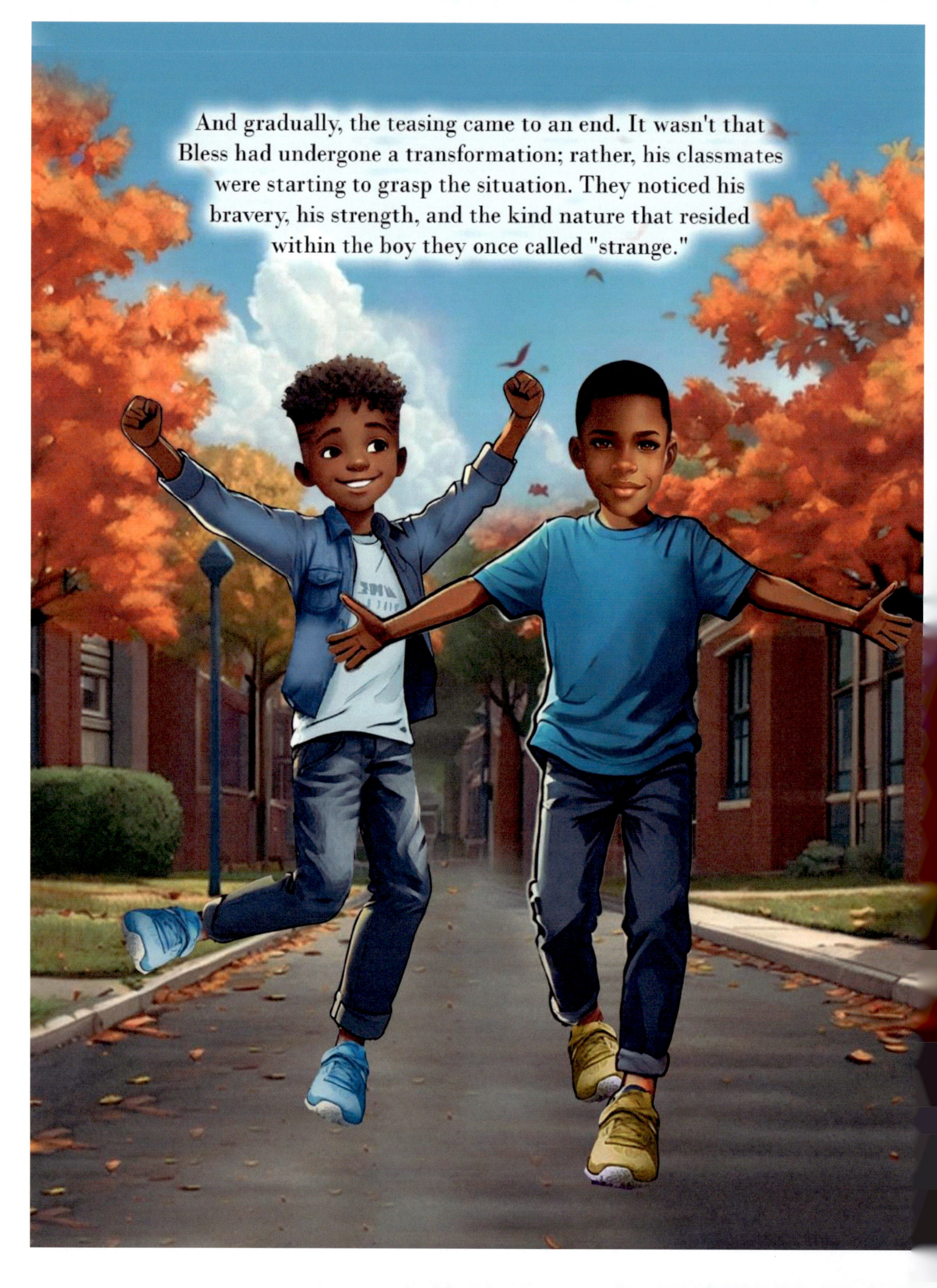

And gradually, the teasing came to an end. It wasn't that Bless had undergone a transformation; rather, his classmates were starting to grasp the situation. They noticed his bravery, his strength, and the kind nature that resided within the boy they once called "strange."

Jason's inner strength!

Stacey Lloyd Ph.D

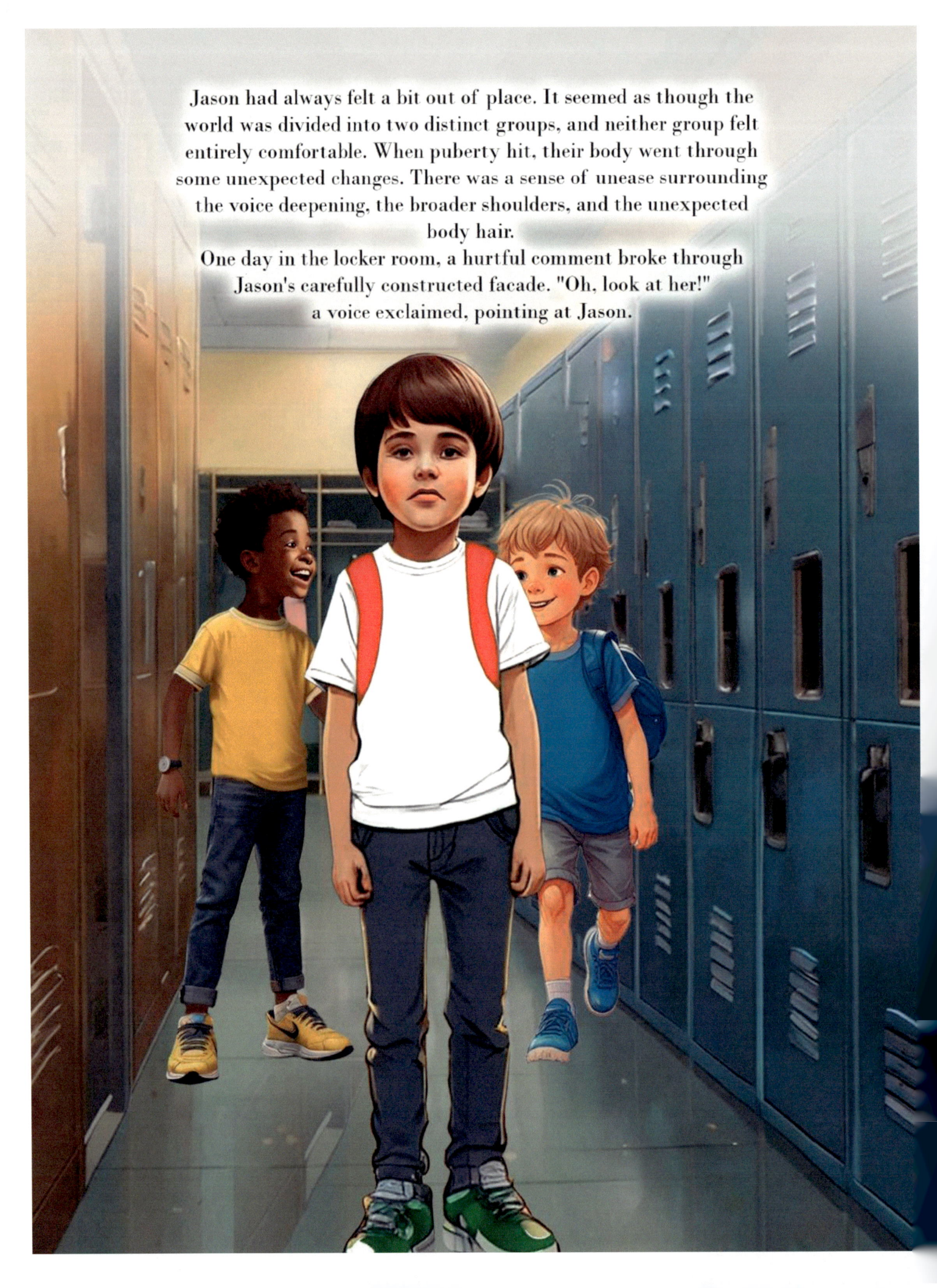

Jason had always felt a bit out of place. It seemed as though the world was divided into two distinct groups, and neither group felt entirely comfortable. When puberty hit, their body went through some unexpected changes. There was a sense of unease surrounding the voice deepening, the broader shoulders, and the unexpected body hair.

One day in the locker room, a hurtful comment broke through Jason's carefully constructed facade. "Oh, look at her!" a voice exclaimed, pointing at Jason.

"Exploring and understanding different gender identities."
The laughter that followed felt surprisingly unkind. From
that point on, the teasing kept getting worse.

Behaving in a way that is not considerate, excluding others, and occasionally resorting to physical aggression. Jason seemed to become more reserved, their once lively personality gradually diminishing.

Attending school became a regular part of their everyday life. Jason was dreading gym class because the locker room was a source of potential embarrassment. Even in the classroom, there were whispers and curious looks that caught people's attention. The world, once full of possibilities, now felt limiting.

During a leisurely afternoon at the library, Jason stumbled upon a captivating book that delved into the topic of gender identity. The words on the page exuded a comforting warmth. Jason was delighted to see a reflection of their own experience for the first time. Despite the challenges, they remained steadfast in their authenticity.

With a warm smile, Jason approached their teacher Mrs. Lloyd. The conversation was engaging, but Mrs. Lloyd listened attentively. She was extremely helpful, offering support, explaining mindfulness, and even connecting Jason with a therapist who specializes in gender identity.

The road ahead appeared challenging. There were more hurtful comments, increased sadness, and stronger feelings of being alone. Surprisingly, Jason stumbled upon a hidden strength that had gone unnoticed until now.

Jason started expressing their true self by wearing clothes that matched their genuine gender identity. Jason went through a gentle change that resulted in a profound feeling of tranquility and fitting in.

Jason found comfort in the constant support of their friend Chris J and Mrs. Lloyd even during the most challenging moments of bullying. They joined the STEM research club at school and found a warm and understanding community. Over time, the world began to transform. Classmates who had once teased were now greeted with smiles. The teachers were kind and made sure to use Jason's correct pronouns.

Jason found comfort in the constant support of their friend Chris J and Mrs. Lloyd even during the most challenging moments of bullying. They joined the STEM research club at school and found a warm and understanding community. Over time, the world began to transform. Classmates who had once teased were now greeted with smiles. The teachers were kind and made sure to use Jason's correct pronouns.

Chris J's Magnificent Mind
A Journey Through Emotions

Stacey Lloyd Ph.D

Chris J loved spending afternoons with his friend Devonte, drawing pictures in the park. One day, Chris J was feeling on top of the world. He had passed his math test and his drawing was coming along perfectly.

He clenched his fists and furrowed his brow.

But then, a strong wind blew his drawing sheet away.
Frustration bubbled up inside Chris J.

Devonte noticed his change in mood. "Hey, Chris J, what's wrong?" he asked gently. Chris J explained what happened, his voice tight with anger.

Mrs. Lloyd, who was nearby, overheard their conversation. She smiled warmly and walked over.
"Chris J," Mrs. Lloyd said kindly, "it sounds like you're feeling frustrated. That's okay, everyone feels frustrated sometimes."
Chris J looked up, surprised. "But how do I stop feeling this way?"

Mrs. Lloyd pointed to her head. "The key is right up here, Chris J, in your magnificent mind!" she explained. "Your brain is like a supercomputer, helping you think and feel."
She then explained that Chris J's frustration was a signal, letting him know he was upset about the lost drawing. "Just like we can control our bodies," Mrs. Lloyd continued, "we can also learn to control our emotions with a little practice."

Mrs. Lloyd taught Chris J some calming down techniques. They took slow, deep breaths together, imagining their frustration melting away like snowflakes.

Chris J felt the tension ease from his shoulders.

Devonte joined in, suggesting they draw a new picture together. Chris J smiled. He realized that even though Chris J felt frustrated, he could choose how to react.

Together, they created an even more fantastic drawing, filled with vibrant colors and their favorite superheroes. Chris J beamed with pride.

He had used his magnificent mind to navigate his emotions and create something wonderful with his friend.
From that day on, Chris J paid more attention to his feelings. He learned that his emotions were messengers, giving him clues about how he was feeling. And most importantly, he learned that he had the power to manage his emotions and use his brain to create a happy and fulfilling life.

Chris J's

Magnificent Mind tells a story about a bright and inquisitive boy who felt the emotion of frustration and learned that the brain is a supercomputer that helps us think and feel and allows us to make positive choices for a more fulfilling life.

Made in the USA
Columbia, SC
29 November 2024